# LIFE HACKS

## Free & Easy Life Hacking Methods To Simplify Your Life

## MEG SMOLINSKI

Let's face it. Every day, it seems like we have more and more to do and less and less time to do it in. Responsibilities pile up, and sometimes it's hard to get through them all. Things start slipping and soon, we've put off tasks that we know we should do for weeks. So how do you keep up with it all? By doing things smarter!

People are always asking me how I get as much done as I do. A lot of it is having a busy schedule and making every moment count. But how do you get the most out of the time that you have? This book is full of tips and tricks that I've gathered over the years, and some "ah-ha!" moments of my own that have streamlined my work and life. I'm happy to share these "life hacks" with you to help you accomplish more in your life as well, and live a happier, healthier way.

# CONTENTS

# CHAPTER 1

## Life Hacks for your home

More often than not, you have more than enough things on your hands when you come home from work. The checklist of things to do never seems to be completed. After a hard day's work and a long commute, it can be nearly impossible to find the energy to clean your house. Most days, all I can think of is sitting down, or better yet, going straight to bed some days! But there are ways to lighten the load and give your home a fresh makeover. For starters, don't feel that you have to everything all at once or every day. Break it down, and start incorporating some of the things below into your routine, and you'll see a difference in your home.

## YOUR LIVING ROOM

Over the years, your walls might start to smell like food, cigarettes, or an "old house." The problem could get even worse if you have a pet. It can be hard to get rid of the animal smell when it sticks to the wall. You don't need to spend a fortune on expensive chemicals. Just wipe down walls and furniture with a mixture of one part white vinegar and eight parts water to remove bad odors from your home. You can do this on painted walls and even wallpaper, as long as you wring out the sponge or rag well.

Do you have pets or children who cause your rugs to move? In order to keep your rug or carpet in place, attach a Velcro strip on the carpet and a Velcro strip on the floor. This little trick will keep the rug in place. Velcro strips have sticky adhesive on the back, so you can basically stick them anywhere and I've found that this works much better than the rubbery mats you can purchase to go under rugs to reduce slippage.

If your furniture has damages and scratches, you will find the unlikely solution to your problem in the form of a walnut. Simply rub a walnut on the surface of the furniture so that the walnut oil could help restore the flawless look of your wooden furniture.

Dryer sheets can make a great duster for your baseboards and the corners of your hardwood floors. For some reason, I find the dust bunnies and hair seems to stick better to dryer sheets than to a regular dusting rag.

Label all of the many cords running from your electronics to the wall so that if you need to unplug something, you don't have to trace it all the way back to the source. You can do this two ways, first by color coding the cord where it goes into the machine and where it goes into the wall. Or, you can take some of the twist-ties next to the bulk bins at your grocery store. They have an extra wide tab for writing, so write down "TV," or "Xbox," and twist it around the cord where it plugs into the wall.

## THE KITCHEN

I love finding hacks for the kitchen. Any and every way to make my food better, tastier, and healthier is fine by me!

For iced coffee in the summer, or to cool down coffee that's too hot, you can add ice cubes, but that waters down your coffee. Instead of using water, make ice cubes out of coffee to keep your coffee strong. Or, make ice cubes out of your favorite creamer for a ice cold treat

At the end of a dinner, you may have just a bit of wine left over. Don't let it go to waste! Freeze it in your ice cube trays, and then add one or two to the next sauce or to use as basting juices for a roast. It saves money, and can add a ton of flavor.

You can do the same thing with bits of left over sauce. Some of these can be packed with flavor and can really enhance your meal.

I know I won't have a healthy snack if it takes effort. I will reach for chips or cookies or some other convenience food. In order to make it easier on myself, I prep fresh fruits and veggies by cleaning and cutting them up all at once. Then I put them in bowls at eye-level in the fridge. It makes it much more likely that I will reach for the bag of carrots or container of apple slices if I see it right away instead of tucked away in a drawer.

Normally, you would throw away the rinds of cheeses such as parmesan. Instead, add them to your next pot of soup or sauce. They will add a lovely amount of creaminess and salt to your soup.

If you need drawer organizers, you can spend money on the fancy plastic ones from the store, or you can repurpose boxes from your recycling bin. Boxes from macaroni and cheese are good size. Just carefully cut the face of the box off. You can even wrap them in colored paper to add some pizzazz to your drawers.

If you are like me, you've ended up with many more reusable grocery bags than you will ever need. Keep some in your car so that you don't have to remember to bring them to the store. Keep the nylon bags that can roll up so small in your glove compartment. Or, if you still have way too many, you can donate them to your local food pantry. If they can give away reusable bags for their food, that helps them cut down on costs from buying bags.

I hate the expense of buying an exotic spice for a new recipe that I am making. More often than not, I use a tiny amount for that one recipe, and then never use again. Instead of going right out to buy it, I ask around in my group of friends first. A lot of them enjoy cooking as much as I do, so there's a good chance that they may have it. In exchange, I usually make a double recipe and give them some of what I've made. This has become a fun food exchange, and it's an exciting surprise to see what we will make for each other.

You can clean your coffee pot with plain white vinegar. It's really a workhorse when it comes to cleaning! Mix equal parts water and vinegar, and brew it as you would coffee -- minus the coffee. Then brew two pots of regular water to rinse it clean and get rid of the vinegar smell.

Going out to eat with friends can break your budget, especially if you all end up splitting the bill no matter what you order. The next time your friend suggests dinner, how about indulging in a dessert and coffee instead? It's not something that we usually treat ourselves to, and splitting a rich dessert and a cup of coffee is so satisfying. It can also be at least half the cost of going out to dinner. If you really want a full meal, consider going out for lunch instead of dinner, which is often cheaper.

An even cheaper way of "going out" is to go on an exercise date. Why do we go out with our friends anyway? To chat and catch up. Sometimes it's hard to do that in a crowded, noisy restaurant. Instead, suggest a walk around the block with your neighbor or meet your friend at a local park. We all need a little bit of extra exercise and a taste of nature, too.

If you are a working parent, you will be surprised by how much time you will save by cooking your meals in advance. Cook meals in bulk, and store them properly in your fridge. You can do this on weekends so that you don't have to worry about meals as you work, and you can also have your kids help and be a part of the project. To make it easy to incorporate lots of fresh vegetables in your diet, do all the vegetable prep (peeling/slicing/etc) in one fell swoop once per week, so you can grab them during the week as a snack or side dish. Think about a restaurant: they have the sous chefs all prepare the basic ingredients in bulk early in the day so they're ready for the dinner rush.

## Cleaning

Cleaning the kitchen and doing the laundry can be two of the most taxing things that you need to do in order to maintain your home. Here are some tips that can help make your tasks easier.

An inexpensive scrub can be made by mixing baking soda or finely ground salt with a bit of water. It will lift off the stains, and then you can rinse with water mixed with a bit of lemon juice for a nice fresh scent. This works really well on sinks and tubs!

You can easily clean stains on coffee and tea mugs by rubbing them with lemon peel and salt. This combination is powerful against dirt and stains.

If you use a blender or a food processor, you don't need to scrub and wash the container. Simply "blend" or "process" a few drops of dishwashing liquid along with half a cup of water. Let the machine clean itself for you! You don't need to exert effort anymore. All you have to do is press a button.

Cleaning up an explosion in the microwave can be daunting. If it's a dried-on mess, put a container of water in the microwave and heat it for one minute. This will add water vapor to the microwave and loosen the food, so you can wipe it right off with a sponge. You can then kill germs on your wet sponge by popping it in the microwave for 30 seconds to disinfect it. Just make sure that it's not dry, as then it might burn.

If you want to prevent glasses and silverware from breaking by knocking against one another, try putting a rubber band around each one to cushion them from each other.

You can also put old newspapers at the bottom of the trash bag in the bin to absorb leftover food juices and odors and keep your trash cans clean and dry. When you take out the garbage, you can put the old ones in the recycling and toss in some new ones. This will prevent any sort of liquid from creating a mess in your kitchen, like when you set the bag on the floor to tie it closed.

## LAUNDRY

Adding a quarter cup of white vinegar to the wash can get rid of tough odors that wouldn't normally wash out. Also, adding a few drops of eucalyptus oil or tea tree oil to a load of sheets or handkerchiefs when you have a cold can help you breathe easier.

If you want to get rid of odor in shoes, the best way to do so is to simply stuff them with a teabag. You can also put teabags in your clothing drawers to use as sachets.

Color-coding towels, bath cloths, and other bathroom items can help your kids keep track of what is theirs as well. This includes each child's hamper to encourage them to help with the laundry by making sure things go in the hamper when they should. Or, if you have one collection area for laundry, purchase a dark-colored hamper for darks and a light-colored or white one for whites. This can help everyone in the house pre-sort the laundry so you don't have to!

One of my favorite tricks is what I call the Hanger Trick. In your closet, if you are wondering what you wear and what you should donate, turn all of the hangers around the opposite way. After you wear an item, launder the item, and put it back in the closet, put the hanger back the normal way. After a few weeks, or at the end of the season, you can easily see which items still have their hangers turned around, and then you can determine what you want to keep and what you want to donate.

My most recent hack both saves me money and saves my nose. I cut up old t-shirts to use as handkerchiefs. The older the shirt, the softer the material and when I have a cold or allergies, it helps to not irritate my nose. It saves me money, because I can just toss them in the laundry and it saves the environment, too, by reusing an old item and reducing waste. I use an old tissue box for the dirty ones, so I'm not always walking through the house to toss them in the hamper. There are lots of uses for old t-shirts - they make great dust rags and polishing rags, and you can make sachets from them with tea or dried herbs. I even use one to dry my hair instead of a towel, because they are much more absorbent.

## Your Bedroom

Looking for ways to tidy up your bedroom? Here are some tips that could help you do it in a jiffy and make your bedroom the oasis it is meant to be.

You will be surprised by how much you can maximize space. For example, walls are never just for pictures and posters. You can simply hang hooks on walls and then use them to store your bags, purses, scarves, and other accessories. Get creative and turn it into a work of art!

Don't ignore the space behind doors too. Hanging stuff behind your doors is ideal for storing things that you pick up just before leaving your home. I especially like hanging a full length mirror and my necklaces on the inside doors of my wardrobe so I can finish off my outfit before walking out the door. Things that are easily seen are easily worn.

We know how difficult it is to have clothes for different seasons. Rotating clothing can help you get ready faster in the morning. If you know it's too warm for your winter clothes, put them away to reduce clutter, and you won't be searching through them to find your summer blouse. Just bring them out when the temperature drops again.

Use chair pockets to help you organize your things. This is ideal for storing stationery, office supplies, children's toys, and other things that you often use. You can hook your chair pocket to your wall for easier access.

Adding shelving, however small or skinny, can help maximize and organize the space in your closet. Adding two bars instead of just the standard one can help you organize tops and bottoms and maximize even more space.

I used to have to hunt for sheets because I just tossed everything into my linen closet. Now I use one pillowcase from the set as a bag to hold everything. I just grab that pillowcase and I know everything from the set is in it. No more hunting and sorting!

Your bedroom furniture makes a huge difference in the way your bedroom looks. From the moment you purchase your furniture, try to make sure that you have efficiency in mind. Go for dual-purpose furniture. For example, choose a mirror that doubles as storage space. Choose a chair that can also be used as a bed in case you have sudden guests who need to sleepover.

## GETTING A GOOD NIGHT'S SLEEP

Keeping your bedroom as a haven just for sleep will help you sleep better in there. Try not to do work or watch TV in bed. If you use your bed mostly for sleep, then it will help signal your body it is time to rest.

Cut down on the caffeine in the afternoon. It can stay in your body for hours and make it hard to decompress at night. When the dreaded afternoon slump hits, take a walk, or replace your office chair with an exercise ball or standing desk to get the blood pumping.

Having a bedtime routine also lets your body know that it's time to calm down to sleep. Each person is different, but sipping a nightly cup of tea, having a bath or shower at the end of the day, dimming the lights, and turning off devices can all be part of the ritual of getting ready for bed, and can help you decompress. Spending the extra time getting ready for bed will pay off in the quality and amount of sleep you get.

Meditation is a great way to relax as well, but many of us try it, think we are doing it wrong, and stop due to frustration. We think, "I'll never get the hang of this," and give up. I encourage you to keep at it and don't think that there is just one way of doing it. Just because you are not totally clearing your mind doesn't mean you aren't helping yourself. Simply taking five to ten minutes to sit quietly without distractions is a good way to take a much-needed break from the day. Start by visualizing something pleasant, like being outside hiking, or watching a sunset. If other thoughts enter your brain, let them go and return to visualizing your outdoor retreat. Breathe deeply when you are doing this and it will help slow your heart rate. As you become more comfortable doing this, add a few minutes at a time.

## THE BATHROOM

Maintaining a clean and functional bathroom is important for your family's hygiene. You don't have to invest in expensive bathroom products just for bathroom maintenance. Here are some of the things you can do to help improve your bathroom.

Did you know that dust builds up on the back of your hairdryer, over the air intake screen? You can easily get rid of this and make the airflow better by using a dry toothbrush on it.

You can use a spice rack for placing your bottled toiletries like hair products and lotions. For a shared bathroom, use coat hooks for storing towels in use. For extra towels, roll them up when you store them, because they then take up less space.

Use small storage solutions to easily find your stuff. Keep big containers under the sink, and refill bottles as needed. Use a magnet strip to line up your bobby pins or hair clips on your mirror.

Get rid of products you don't find yourself using. I know it's hard to throw away something that you potentially spent a lot of money on, but keeping that clutter around the bathroom can be subtly stressful in the morning while you're getting ready. Also, don't keep half empty bottles of products laying around for the same reason. Either use up all that's left in the bottle or tube, or put it in the recycling to get rid of it. To get every last ounce of the product out of a tube, cut the top of the tube off about an inch from the top. This allows you to scoop out the last of the lotion. Replace the top over the cut bottom, and slide it down to keep it from drying out.

Using sponges to apply foundation instead of your hands can lead to less acne, as our hands are full of bacteria. They also help you blend the makeup really well.

My hair ties tend to end up everywhere, and sometimes my cats will find them and play with them. I solved this problem by putting them all on a twist-tie to keep them together. Or, you can install a wall hook and hang them next to the mirror to organize them.

If you're wondering how best to spend your money on makeup, splurge on items that will be close to your skin, such as foundation, concealer, and moisturizers. Save money by buying less expensive color items, such as eye shadow and lip color. These items change seasonally, and you can keep up with the new fashion cheaper this way.

Keep your makeup brushes clean to prevent a buildup of bacterial and possible acne as that bacteria transfers to your skin. Use a gentle soap and some water, and then hang them up to dry. How? If they have a hold in the handle, you can make a hook from a paper clip and hang them on a hanger in the bathroom. If they don't, use a binder clip or chip clip to attach them to the hanger.

If your hair doesn't have its normal healthy bounce and shine, you don't need a product to combat this problem. Instead, you probably need to use less - unless you have very thin or fine hair, you don't need to wash your hair every day. Your scalp makes its own healthy oils for your hair, and allowing them to penetrate your hair by not washing them away will improve the look and feel of your hair. It may take one or two days to transition, but it is worth it. Instead of washing daily, you can simply rinse it or only use conditioner in between washings.

## YOUR GARAGE AND YARD

Don't make the mistake of ignoring your garage. If your garage is full and cluttered, it makes you less likely to want to start new projects. When finding the right tools for the job is a job in and of itself, it can sap your motivation. Make your garage organized and welcoming with these tips.

The most basic practice that you can do to keep your garage clean is to avoid storing everything in there. Go ahead and throw away the non-essentials.

Simple curtains can do wonders in making your garage look a bit homey, and helps hide valuables that thieves might be interested in. Installing a motion sensor light can be a good idea as well.

To store your things in the garage, it is a good idea to build a vertical shelf where you can store your tools, sporting goods, and other materials. Everything that can be hung on the walls should be, to prevent piles of things you have to sort through. Piles take up a lot of room, too, which may prevent you from having enough space to actually park your car in your garage.

One thing that you should watch out for is how you park your car in your garage. Use pool noodles to cushion the walls against accidental bumps on your car. Cut and drill pool noodles onto the walls of your garage to cushion those blows to your car doors. This will allow you to save a ton of money on paint jobs.

Yard work will go faster and in fact, be safer, if your tools are properly maintained. Sharpen them once a year. A sharp tool cuts cleanly and quickly, and requires less effort that may lead to you cutting yourself. Also sanitize them with a 10% bleach solution in between uses to make sure that any diseases present in your yard aren't spread. If you lend them out, sanitize them when they are returned to you, because you don't necessarily know how they were used. Keep a spray bottle of sanitizing solution in the garage clearly labeled to make it easier.

If you have a project that needs a specific tool you don't have, see if your neighbor has it, instead of wasting money on something you will only use once. Or, see if your neighborhood has a "tool library" where you can check things out for a certain project. Maybe you and your neighbors can start your own!

One of the simplest ways to maintain a green lawn is to not mow as frequently. Mowing frequently puts a lot of stress on the grass plant, not just with the cutting action of the mower, but also by walking on it so much. A longer grass leaf will look greener, and the plant will be healthier so it can fight off disease on its own, instead of needing a chemical.

If you are having a big event at your house, or you are looking to sell your house, investing in mulch is a great way to make things look shipshape. Spreading mulch on your flower beds and tree beds really spruces up the house and increases curb appeal.

## LASTLY...

One of the best ways to simplify your life is to get rid of the amount of stuff we all have. It collects over the years, and sometimes we don't even notice it building up until it overwhelms us. Decluttering your home can make it feel new again, and is a great family project. It can also uncover a lot of things you didn't know you had and can use again. Make a pile of things that should be thrown away because they are too damaged to use. Some things may be able to be repaired, but ask yourself if you really will repair it and use it again. If not, get rid of it, or it will just become clutter again. Sorting out things to donate to charity will show your kids that giving to others is a great idea.

# CHAPTER 2
## Life Hacks For Your Office

A cluttered desk can really decrease your productivity and make your office ever more stressful. It can be a put off for others who visit your office. People may assume that you don't work productively because of the state of mess on your desk. You will be a more productive employee if you are in a happy environment, where you can find everything easily, and people can see that you pay attention to the details. If you are more productive, you have a better chance of becoming successful in your career.

**Staying fit:** Sitting on a chair all day can do damage to your body in the long run. Get some exercise simply by replacing your chair with a large exercise ball. Move around every so often. Stretch so that your body will get some movement. If you can get a standing desk, that would be perfect.

**Toilet paper rolls to organize cords:** With toilet paper rolls, you'll be surprised at how easy it is to avoid tangles. Just store the cords vertically in the toilet paper rolls. If you want, you can even wrap or color the rolls in any way you want in order to make them more presentable.

**Sticky notes to clean your keyboard:** When your keyboard is full of dust and crumbs, you will have a difficult time typing. A simple way to clean your keyboard is to simply use the adhesive side of a sticky note. Insert it in the spaces between keys and the dirt will automatically stick to it. It's more hygienic than blasting air in the keyboard, which blows the dust and crumbs and germs all over your desk.

**Or use a toothbrush:** Another way to clean out the keyboard is to use an old toothbrush to get in between the cracks.

**Adhesive wall hooks to mount your tablet:** You can use plastic hooks to mount your tablet like a television.

Buy a few, and carefully position them so that your tablet could comfortably sit on them when you want to watch something or use your table as a computer with a Bluetooth keyboard.

**Smartphone ruler:** It is a good idea to take a photo of a ruler. Edit it to ensure that it is aligned properly. You can use this when you have a sudden need to measure something.

**Presentations:** Remember, for all visual presentations, white text with black outline is easier to read. Make sure that the font size you choose is appropriate. Avoid confusing fonts, and just stick to what looks professional. Also, don't bombard your presentation with words. Stick to keywords that will help get your points across.

**Make Friends:** Secretaries, tech support, and janitors are the true power in an office. Making friends, remembering birthdays, and saying hello will go a long way!

**Stress management:** Whether at home or in the office, stress management largely involves taking care of your body. Take deep breaths when you feel yourself getting overwhelmed; this will help slow down your heart rate and get you back on track. Walk around when you're on the phone so that you'll get the blood pumping and a little exercise while you can. Avoid overeating when you're out working or travelling. Also, keep in mind that what you eat greatly affects your mood. While we may feel that we deserve a "treat" because we have been working so hard, still make healthy choices when indulging. Get a small size, ask for less sugar, and split a dessert with a friend. This will help prevent that dreaded afternoon slump.

**Find cords easily:** How many times have you unplugged your phone from its charging cord, only to have the cord slip back behind the desk? I hate fishing around for it among all the other cords, so I clipped a binder clip to the back edge of my desk. Now the top of the cord is always there, ready for me to plug in my phone.

**Goal Setting:** Set little daily goals to help you achieve the things you want. This is especially true when facing a big project or challenge, or even a test. Try to tackle a little each day, but still give yourself some flexibility in case something unexpected comes up. By hitting small goals, you can motivate yourself to keep going and see the successes piling up.

**Positive Energy:** It is always a good idea to surround yourself with positive people who will bring out the best in you. Toxic and negative people can bring you down. They will make you feel uninspired, and you will likely end up unhappy if negative people are always surrounding you.

**Resumes:** Every time something happens which you think will improve your chances of getting a job, update your resume as soon as possible. This is easier and more manageable than trying to update it only when a new opportunity comes along, and will help you move quickly to secure that new job or promotion. It shows potential employers that you're organized and think ahead.

**Keep a "Yay me!" file:** Whenever I received a great thank-you email or note, I always printed it off and kept it in a separate file. When things got tough, I used it as positive reinforcement that I knew what I was doing and I was good at my job. Also, when it came time to ask for a promotion or update my resume, I could easily pull out my list of accomplishments to reference.

**Don't multitask:** While multitasking is giving you the illusion that you are achieving a lot, you are actually not. You are constantly shifting from one task to another. Every time you shift your attention, your brain takes a bit of time to adjust. When your brain is completely focused on achieving something, you are actually able to achieve more in a short amount of time. Rather than trying to achieve multiple things at once, focus your brain on finishing one task before moving on to the next. It is not as difficult as you think!

If you want to focus, it is best to work in an environment where you are most productive. Make sure that you have a work area with all the things you need to remove all unwanted distractions. The single biggest distraction is our phone - turn it completely off if you want to concentrate, not just on "silent" mode. Put it in a drawer or another room if you have to. Download items you need to review or edit and then turn your device on airplane mode to help keep you focused.

**Not everything is urgent:** When you receive e-mails in the middle of the day, don't feel the need to respond immediately. The truth is that you don't really have to, unless it is really a matter of life and death. You don't even have to read everything you receive. Follow a rough outline of how you want your day to go, and don't let petty e-mails distract you. Have an automatic reply that says, "I am away from my computer and will return to respond to you emails at 2:00 p.m.," or something along those lines. Encourage people to call with questions, as this is often faster than long email responses.

**Start early:** If you are a company employee, you pretty much have no other choice but to follow your company schedule. It would help if you start coming to work at least fifteen minutes before your actual work hours to jumpstart your brain. It does not matter what you do in your office. The important thing is to give yourself time to transition into work mode before actually starting. Asking for a flexible start time is a great perk if your company is not in the position to give raises. Think outside the box when it comes to perks that could help you be a better employee.

**Diffuse a tense situation:** If you receive an email that comes across as negative or critical, it can be our first impulse to send back a nasty email. That often serves no purpose but to escalate things. Instead, take the time to write the response to get it out of your system, but <u>don't</u> send it. Let it sit in your drafts for a few hours or even until the end of the day. Then, reread the email, make adjustments, and send a response. Or, wait until the end of the day and walk out with the person to talk about things before heading out for the day. Often, conversations in person are more collegial that over email.

**Stop working:** Sometimes, if you spend too much time working on something, your productivity suffers too. It's not always about the length of time you worked. It's also about how productive you are. Give yourself enough time to rest. You are only human, and you can only achieve so much. Don't over-commit and burn yourself out.

**Go on a real vacation:** If you are going to be away from the office for vacation, make sure you really do take a break by turning on your out of office reply and not checking your email. Disconnect your email from your phone for the length of your vacation so you are not tempted to look at it. When you set the end date, set it for a day later than you are scheduled to get back into the office. That will give you a day to catch up on things before people expect a response. It creates less stress, and then people are always happy to receive an answer before they expect one! If you <u>do</u> need to check in while you are on vacation, make a phone call to check in halfway through. You can put out any fires or assure people you will complete the task as soon as you are back in the office. If you email, you run the risk of getting wrapped up in a long email chain.

**Use repetition techniques:** When you say something out loud, it will be easier for your brain to recall information. For example, when you are introduced to Gina, greet her with a phrase like, "Nice meeting you, Gina. Gina is a beautiful name." Try to repeat the name multiple times in your conversation. Repeating the name again and again will embed it in your memory.

**Use your own mnemonics:** Mnemonics, or patterns of letters, words, or phrases, are a good way to remember things. If you use mnemonics, you are actually using your various senses to remember information. This makes it much easier for the brain to process and recall information. Use your own sense of humor to remember things well. Construct positive images that can help you to remember the important information that you need.

**Train your brain:** Train your brain to think more using exercises such as puzzles and board games. Playing scrabble, crossword, and Sudoku could do wonders for your brain. You can also play memory games that will keep your brain working. The more you train your brain, the more efficient it will become. Simple games like these can even help prevent Alzheimer's and other brain diseases.

**Engage your senses:** The more senses you involve in learning something new, the easier it will be for you to remember important information later on. It would be best if you know what kind of learner you are. Some people learn faster through body movement, some by imagining pictures, and some by singing songs. For visual learners, you can translate text into pictures. For auditory learners, you can assign a song or a tune, which can make learning faster and more efficient. Try to discover what kind of learner you are, so that you can maximize your own learning process.

**Write it down:** Whenever you have the luxury to write things down, go ahead and do so. The physical act of writing embeds the important details into your memory, regardless of whether you ever look back at the note. Handwriting also engages the brain more fully than typing on a keyboard and locks things into your memory better than using a screen.

**Clear clutter:** How many of us sign up for e-newsletters we never read? If you sign up for e-newsletters, make sure you are unsubscribing if they don't add anything to your life. If you don't, you're just doing pointless busy work by reading them or having to delete them. I usually give each one three issues and if I don't get anything out of them in three tries, I unsubscribe.

**Delegate tasks:** You have to accept that no matter how good you are, you cannot do everything and also, there are others who can do certain tasks better than you can. Part of being a good leader is knowing how to delegate tasks effectively. You need to be able to "let go" of tasks that you can have someone else do. If you're unsure of how to choose which tasks can be let go, learn from President Eisenhower and his task delegation matrix. It works great and can be seen here: https://timegt. com/2010/07/14/what-is-the-eisenhower-matrix/

**Meeting time:** When you are in a meeting, it is easy to get carried away by talking about ideas and details. However, you must keep in mind that meetings are often for discussions rather than for action. Learn to keep meetings short and productive. Have an agenda people can reference to stay on track. Talk about the things that need to be done, and try to get directly to the point. Avoid lengthy and unnecessary discussions. Assign action items to be completed before the next meeting. My best tip though is to remove all the chairs in the room. This has been a proven method to significantly cut down on the time that people spend in meetings as nobody wants to stand for an hour long meeting!

**Leave the office:** The occasional late night is perfectly acceptable and often necessary. Staying in the office after work hours is a sign of dedication and commitment. However, if you do this all the time, you will burn yourself out. Also, leaving your office on time gives yourself a personal deadline that ensures THAT you maximize your eight hours at work. If you know that you need to complete everything before going home, it is more likely that you will be pressured to maximize your work hours.

**Ask questions:** Do not feel insecure about not knowing how to perform certain tasks. Even company leaders don't know every single step of the workflow, so don't be afraid to ask. The worst thing you can do in a job is to pretend that you know something that you really have no idea about. Part of growing as an employee is learning to accept your weaknesses, and learning how to make them strengths.

**Follow the two-minute rule:** If you can complete a task in two minutes, do it immediately so they don't pile up. If, however, you have a task that will take more than an hour, take time to schedule when you will complete that task. That will make your schedule more organized. Thus, no time is wasted and no task is skipped.

**Say "no" sometimes:** You don't need to accept every single task that you are assigned to you. Part of a being a good employee is knowing how and when to say no to certain tasks. If you feel that you are doing too much or if something is outside the scope of your knowledge, know how to say "no." Good employers will not hold it against you if you do not agree to everything. In fact, there are some who might even see it as a strong point.

**Centralize your information:** This advice is applicable for all kinds of documents. You must put all information together in an easy-access centralized folder. This will make it easier to come up with information in case the need arises. However, don't compromise the security of your documents. Make sure that when you centralize your information, it is also well secured and protected.

**Review schedules weekly:** Every Sunday, review the upcoming week with the other members of your family. This lessens the chance of forgetting something and reminds people of responsibilities. This helps *tremendously* with making everyone's lives sync better and it helps keep the lines of communication open.

# CHAPTER 3

## Travel Hacks

Travel can be a fun experience. however, if you do not prepare, it can be taxing and stressful. There are a million things that could go wrong when you leave your home. Part of the fun of traveling is experiencing the unexpected, but when too many things go wrong, it turns into a nightmare instead of a vacation. Even seasoned travelers make mistakes too, so the first tip is to not get in a panic when something goes wrong and to do some simple prep work to help prevent any problems. Hopefully the tips below can help you avoid unnecessary trouble.

First, always pack the night before as much as possible. you never know what the morning can bring, so be as ready as possible before your big trip. I didn't hear my alarm for one trip, and woke up incredibly late. I was able to toss the last couple of items in my suitcase, throw on my clothes, and bolt out the door because I had everything sitting out. I made the plane, but it was a close call, and I hope that never happens again!

Setting two alarm clocks before a morning flight is a good idea. Better safe than sorry.

Make a checklist. Don't forget to pack everything that you need. If you are under any kind of medication, you must remember to pack enough medicine for your trip, and I usually pack a few extra doses as well, just in case. You wouldn't want to go running around pharmacies, especially in a foreign country. It can be difficult to explain what you need, and dosages of their tablets might be different. Also, try to pack basic medicines for headaches, fever, and colds.

When you pack your clothes, instead of folding your clothes, try rolling them, as this technique has proven to be very effective in saving space. Bring classic pieces, and just mix and match when you are at your destination. Even if you are going to a tropical island for vacation, it is always a good idea to bring a nice dress or a smart casual outfit just in case something comes up.

A great tip is to take a photo of each suitcase while it's open so that you have an image of what's in each suitcase. That way when you land, you won't be searching for which suitcase has diapers—this is a great tip for traveling with kids!

If you are going for a short trip, you can use straws as containers for creams and liquids. Just make sure to seal them well and to put them in a ziplock to avoid making a mess in your luggage.

Hotels are often pricey. If you are looking for something more affordable, try looking for a house for rent (if you are traveling with family) or a room for rent (if you are travelling alone). This has the added benefit of saving you money, because you can cook your own food instead of going out to eat. I love exploring foreign markets and grocery stores as well to see how they differ from home. Even if you do prefer to go out to eat, at the very least, you can have a quick breakfast or pack a lunch at the house or apartment before heading out for the day.

Ever go on a long trip and come back and can't remember where the heck you parked your car? Take a quick photo with your smartphone BEFORE you leave the parking garage of which level and parking spot you used.

Make sure that you scan your passport, visa, and ticket, and email them to yourself. You can also memorize your passport number and flight details if possible. This small step can save you from stress in case you lose these very important travel documents.

If you are going to a foreign-speaking country, search for apps that could help you to communicate with the locals. You don't need to learn the entire language. Choose a few key works, such as "toilet" or "please" and "thank you." Being polite in the local language means a lot to people.

When you plan to bring your camera, do not forget to take a picture of yourself first. It will prove that the camera is yours in case you lose it.

Always remember the address of where you are staying. It is wise to bring a card of the hotel with you in case you get lost. You can always just show the card to someone, and it will be easier for you to find your way home.

While some countries often give tax rebates or discounts to tourists, there are vendors and sellers who will take advantage of tourists who are not informed of the proper pricing. While bartering isn't as common in the U.S., it's very common in other countries, and the price on the tag is not necessarily the price of the item. Also, in Europe, be sure to look for a blue VAT FREE symbol in a shop—depending on the country and what you're buying, you could save 19% off the purchase price!

When you travel around tourist spots, one of the easiest ways to save money is to bring bottled water. You are bound to get thirsty often if you are always walking. Just refill your bottle whenever you get a chance.

One great app to use is CityMaps2Go—it's free, and you can download a Google-based city map of most major cities. You don't need a data plan to run the app and it works as a GPS too! Plus, you'll have Wikipedia articles at your fingertips in the app so that you can do your own walking tour of the city.

Purchase an extra phone power cord and store it in your suitcase so you'll never forget it. Sometimes, hotels have extra cords to lend if you do forget it, though.

Order free samples of toiletries to take on trips instead of buying expensive travel sizes of your favorite products. If you need a tiny amount of something, squirt it into a contact lens container and label it with a marker.

If you are traveling with gifts, don't wrap them until you get to your destination, as airport security can open them to inspect them. Bring the paper with you and wrap it once you get to your destination. Also, I often grab free street and highway maps when they are available, as they fold up nicely for this, and they make pretty interesting wrapping paper. You can even personalize it by using a map of the recipient's hometown or home state.

Make sure to stay hydrated while you are traveling. More often than not, you are doing more walking than you normally do in your day when you are on vacation and dehydration can sneak up on you and make you feel terrible. Especially keep an eye on your water intake if you are in high temperatures or high humidity.

Make sure to rest, too. Will you really enjoy and take in the things you are seeing if you are too tired to care? Plan and prioritize your day. You don't always need to see everything in the museum you are visiting. Just hit the highlights, and don't wear yourself out. This is supposed to be vacation and a rest!

# CONCLUSION

Life is stressful enough as it is. You can find ways to reduce your own stress by being creative and innovative. You don't have to know everything, you don't have to have the solution to everything, and you certainly don't need to do things the same way everyone else does! All you need to do is to try to minimize your day-to-day stress with life hacks, simple solutions to everyday problems, and use what works for you in your home and office. Life hacks will make your life surprisingly easier. They will allow you to navigate around difficult situations with little stress and hassle, not to mention the satisfaction of coming up with your own creative solution to a problem. Whether you are at home or in the office, you can use life hacks to be a more efficient and reliable person. Life hacks do not need to be expensive. In fact, the things you need might be right within your reach.

At home, you can use life hacks in completing your household tasks. In your office, you can use life hacks to become a more productive employee. When you travel, you can use various life hacks too. You can use life hacks in almost any area of your life. You can even come up with your own life hacks if you wish. You just need to be creative and the sky is the limit!

I hope you've found at least a handful of useful tips and tricks in this book. If you have, don't keep it to yourself; share it with a review on Amazon and tell your friends about your new-found knowledge! Maybe this will even inspire to you to come up with great hacks of your own!

# The Coaching Secret

# Secret

–

# The Ugly Truth

M A. GRANT

ISBN-10: 1514189291
ISBN-13: 978-1514189290

British Library Catalogue in Publication Data:
A catalogue record for this book is available from the British Library.

www.the-leadership-secret.com